Table of Contents

What this book is about?

BLACK BOYS, BOYS of African-descent, are in a crisis! While there are countless success stories to hold up as examples of what our boys can become, there are exponentially more that point to the fact that many have lost their way. Whether it be the statistics on the number of black men ending up in prison, or the success rates of black boys compared to black girls, or the salary rates of black males when compared to other demographic groups in our society – there is a crisis and there has been for some time.

Even sadder is the fact that many of our boys did not start with an level playing field; the chips were stacked against them from the off. Why? While there are a multitude of reasons - social, economic, education and environmental that play a part - a big factor in this handicap comes not from them as individuals but from the fact that many had a lack of guidance in their lives and/or lacked high-quality guidance for when they were fortunate enough to have it present. Who should this guidance come from? From us, of course! Whether that be in a direct role as parents or guardians or more indirect roles as relatives and family members, friends and acquaintances and those roles in the wider community and society such as teachers, pastors or coaches.

For those fortunate enough to have high-quality guidance in their lives, the world becomes their oyster, leaving the pearl of their fate and destiny firmly in their hands. This book attempts to lay firmly down what this guidance should look like and what it should consist of. If we want our boys of African-descent to not only succeed but to *thrive* and impact the world around them, the guidance given to them must match that ambition. It must inherently differ from that they receive from the other important social institutions that they download information from. We must tell them things that the schools will not. We must instruct them spiritually in ways that the church cannot. We must parent them in ways that our parents and fore-parents did not know how.

As its title states, this book is meant as a handbook. An instructional manual that can be used as a reference in its entirety or in parts to systematically understand and deliver a method of instruction to unlock the inner brilliance of our boys of African-descent. Each chapter is directed at providing an aspect of the keys needed to unlock this inner brilliance but as with all things, any key is useless if not applied to the correct lock and in the correct manner. It is hoped that for those that read the book, that they recognize the power they can play in unlocking the brilliance of our Suns (Sons). Although the luminescence of one sun is bright enough to irradiate a whole solar system, it can only be imagined how our world would change and benefit from the radiance of thousands of enlightened ones! The question lies with us - do we have what it takes to yield this power and take on this responsibility!

Principle 1

Nutrition - Provide his body with the most optimal tools it needs to grow and develop.

HUMAN BEINGS ARE living things. Seems obvious right! But, really, how do we know? Well, scientists have denoted seven core features that all living things exhibit - *nutrition, respiration, movement, respiration, excretion, sensitivity, growth, reproduction.* All living things take in **NUTRITION**. Nutrition provides an organism with a source of energy so that all the processes of life can be carried out. All living things **RESPIRE**. That is, they take in oxygen and combine it with glucose in order to release energy that can be used by the organism. All living things exhibit **MOVEMENT**. Movement is essential for living things in order for them to obtain food, compete for resources or to find mates to reproduce. Even plants move. Plants will turn to face the sun so they can get the most amount of light to carry out photosynthesis. All living things **EXCRETE**. Organisms take into their living systems many substances and utilize these substances using various chemical reactions. The resultant end products of these reactions sometimes have to be removed. This is accomplished through the process of excretion. Without excretion, these waste products would accumulate and eventually cause the organism's internal system to malfunction resulting in illness or even death. All living things have some aspect of ***SENSITIVITY*** to their external and internal environment. In this way, they can adjust the conditions of their living system so that it can work optimally by responding to environmental change. All living things **GROW**. Even the smallest bacteria do not spontaneously generate but forms from a process involving cellular growth. Finally, all living things **REPRODUCE**. Reproduction is the penultimate achievement of any and all life forms. It ensures that the unique and priceless genetic material of an organism can be passed on to a new generation who hopefully can continue the cycle of life of your species.

Although ALL these processes are indispensable for any living organism, ***nutrition*** can be seen as one of the most important, if they had to be ranked. Without nutrition, the raw material needed for respiration to occur would not be available and thus no energy would be able to be provided for the other six life processes. As living human beings, this same significance of nutrition applies and becomes even more critical during the developmental years in the life of a young boy of African-descent. Experts have mapped the developmental stages of children and recognized several important milestones in this developmental process.

In the early developmental stages between birth and 12 months, our bodies grow at the quickest rate that they ever will over our lifetime. All the different vital organ systems of the body are included in this fantastic growth spurt and having an optimal nutritional base from which to support this growth is critical during this period. Interestingly, at birth, the head of a child is relatively close in size to that of an adult sized head when compared to the growth that other parts of the body such as the limbs will have to go through. Scientists also know that most of the brain cells we will have as adults are also formed (called neurogenesis) by the time we are born. What this tells us is that much of the development of the brain in terms of growth in size occurs <u>before birth</u>. Although the size of the head and the amount of brain cells we have may not change by much after birth, the forming of new neural pathways in the brain tissue does and in a similar rapid rate to the rest of the body in the first year of growth. This points out the need for nutritional considerations to not only be optimal after a child is born but also straight from the time of initial conception.

The most perfect food during this critical time between birth and 12 months is mother's breast milk which has been shown time and time again in research studies to have countless benefits for a baby during this first year of birth, both in terms of nutrition as well as in other physiological areas of development. Breast milk contains the optimal balance of nutrients that a child needs, and the mother's body changes the milk's composition as the baby develops to ensure that the nutritional and physiological needs are being met. From the initial production of colostrum by the breasts, which see the baby get that first boost in protein and antibodies to the evolution into mature milk which provide the baby with the proteins, fats, sugar and minerals that the baby needs, there is no better food that can support and underpin the development of a baby in its first year of life.

One of the most important areas of the brain's development during a child's first years are in those locations that control motor skills, both gross and fine. These are the skills that allow a child to crawl, eventually walk and also pick up and handle objects in their environment. While these may at first seem basic, it is the ability to accomplish these skills that facilitate a child being able to play and thus investigate the world they are living in. It is through this 'play/investigate cycle' that further pathways in the brain are formed, particularly those that will link into the later stages of brain development that facilitate logic, decision making and critical thinking. Having the correct balance of the five nutrients - proteins, carbohydrates, fats and especially vitamins and minerals - is essential to support the development of the brain tissue and the various other organ systems that are needed for a child to explore its surroundings effectively. A child's skeletal structure must be strong, and their body must have a strong immune system provided by a correct balance of vitamins and minerals to help fight off any pathogens that it may encounter.

From the ages of 1 to 5 years old, the development of the physical ABCs - agility, balance and coordination - is fundamental to setting a strong foundation towards being healthy and physically able in the later stages of a boy's life. Development of the ABCs through play and exercise not only helps fitness and the fine and gross motor skills of the child but it also serves to again create new pathways in the brain. As the brain problem-solves to interpret situations where a child's body is called upon to express agility, balance and coordination, bio-chemical neural pathways can be created and synchronized where they did not previously exist. Again, nutritional considerations are critical so that a child can not only have the energy it needs to exercise and express themself through active play but also so that their body systems can be healthy and strong to robustly deal with the physical stresses that increasingly active play will inevitably bring. If the child's development between birth and 5 can be generalized to characterize more left-brain aspects such as movement and action, the development of a child between 6-11 (pre-puberty) can be seen to shift towards those features that are generally attributed to the right hemisphere and center of the brain (limbic system). These are namely the application of critical thinking, logic (right-brain) and emotions (limbic system). Again, nutritional considerations are important as an imbalance in food group consumption can promote tiredness, a lack of focus and in the long run, poor decision making and a lack of quality of learning.

We all know that the arrival of puberty sees massive changes take place in a boy's physical structure. His body starts to produce massive amounts of hormones like testosterone that promote the growth of muscle and hair. The brain generally has stopped growing new brain tissue except in one specific area - the hippocampus - the area of the brain responsible for memory and learning. This is a critical stage in a male's development as it marks a transition between being a boy and becoming a young man. As a young man, our males need to be able to have not only the physical strength and fitness to protect and serve our black community but also the skill sets and capacity to learn new ones. An emphasis on having a healthy and balanced diet is extremely important at this stage, as over the teenage years as the boy develops into a young man, ideally he should be putting more demands on himself physically and mentally to help him become a strong resource for his family and community, not to mention himself as an individual. Unfortunately, as this also a time when boys become very independent, they are subject to negative influences from the media and peers on what choices they should be making including what they should eat. Eating non-nutritious foods such as fatty snacks, fried foods, foods and drinks high in preservatives and sugars will severely impact their health, particularly their skin, digestive system and immune system, which in turn will impact their ability to think and process information effectively.

From the information above, it can clearly be seen that the optimal development across all the stages of a child's milestones is dependent on supporting the changes within that child's body through effective nutrition. In particular, the healthy development of the muscles, skeleton, lungs, immune system and most critically, the nervous system including the brain, are areas of particular focus in terms of nutrition. Mother's breast milk is the only food that a child in its first year of life needs due to its superior nutritional and bioactive composition. Following on from this, as a child develops teeth and starts to show interest in foods other than mother's milk, a strict focus should be put on the foods highest in vitamins and minerals, the fruits and vegetables, so as to promote the healthy development of the body's diverse organ systems and its intricate parts. High quality protein and fats should also be provided in significant amounts to facilitate the tissue growth and development that the boys' bodies will undergo during that period of their lives.

Those fruits and vegetables that are the easiest to digest and have the highest nutritional density should be focused on such as ripe banana and plantain, avocado, sweet potato, etc. A child should be introduced to water from a young age (after weaning) and sugary, concentrated or salty drinks should not be given as this is the age where habits and becoming accustomed to specific food tastes start to form. As the child gives up breast milk altogether, the emphasis on fruits and vegetables as the largest percentage of a child's diet should be maintained with other foods like meat be given only sparingly if so desired. If meats are desired to be consumed, then an emphasis on healthy choices of meats such as fish and lean meats such as chicken or turkey can be chosen. Any concerns regarding protein and fat consumption from a meat-limited diet can be addressed by the provision of grains, beans, seeds, nuts and oils in their various forms, which are far more nutritionally superior than meats due to their nutrient density.

<u>Recommended foods</u>
Birth - 1: Breast milk

Weaning period: Breast milk, easily digestible soft fruits such as ripe banana, ripe plantain, ripe avocado, ripe mango, vegetables soft after cooking such as baked or boiled sweet potato, baked or boiled pumpkin, boiled dasheen, etc., small amounts of boiled grains especially millet, short-grain brown rice and oats

Toddler: easily digestible soft fruits such as ripe banana, ripe plantain, ripe avocado, ripe mango, vegetables soft after cooking such as baked or boiled sweet potato, baked or boiled pumpkin, boiled dasheen, etc., small amounts of boiled grains especially millet, short-grain brown rice and oats, introduction of nutrient dense vegetables particularly green ones such as cabbage, broccoli, spinach, okra, etc. introduction of nutrient dense protein sources such as soaked and boiled beans and pulses (lentils) and, if desired, lean meats with an emphasis on fresh ocean fish (non-farmed), non-farmed salmon or limited amounts of organic, free range turkey or organic free range chicken

Young boy - Teenager: focus on fruits and vegetables, particularly those vegetables diverse in color (green - broccoli, kale, etc., purples - cabbage, beets and swiss chard, red - tomatoes, and orange - carrots, pumpkin, sweet potato),roots and tubers such as sweet potato and yams, and nutrient dense protein and quality fat sources such as nuts, seeds, soaked and boiled beans and pulses (lentils), and, if desired, lean meats with an emphasis on fresh ocean fish (non-farmed), non-farmed salmon or limited amounts of organic, free range turkey or organic, free range chicken. High consumption of water. Concentrated juices, junk food, preserved and packaged foods and fatty, fried foods to be avoided.

Super foods such as those that boost immunity and healing (like herbal teas), those high in trace minerals such as sea vegetables, kale and sea moss and those traditional foods that have particular unique nutritional benefits such as pure cacao (chocolate) can also be introduced and used over this period.

Principle 2

Reading and Mathematics - Reading and mathematics provides a boy with the ability to access the navigation system that he needs to lay the course for his life.

TEACHING BOYS OF African-descent to read is one of the most important and impactful skills that he can be given. Studies upon studies have shown that a child that reads will do better than those that do not in regard to academic achievement. A 2013 study by the Institute of Education found that children who read for pleasure made more progress in math, vocabulary and spelling between the ages of 10 and 16 than those who generally did not read. Reading as a pleasurable past time during secondary school showed the largest impact on a child development at older ages than influence from their parents. Going to the library regularly was four times greater than the benefits children obtained from having a parent with a degree.[1]

---

[1] *www.literacytrust.org.uk/news/5560_study_provides_evidence_that_reading_for_pleasure_boosts_children_s_academic_performance*

Studies have also shown that reading books and writing are among the brain-stimulating activities shown to slow down old age decline in cognition and contribute to a less rapid rate of memory loss. It is also clear from the research that the earlier that reading is started the greater the impact on a child.[2] Reading also clearly impacts a child's ability to access a wider range of vocabulary.[3] This means that a child who reads will not only be able to express himself better but also be able to understand the expressions and information of others.

Children should be encouraged to read from as early age as possible, even before birth! Speaking to a child is a key precursor to how they form their ability to speak and use language. Reading to a child in the womb has also been researched to show that babies not only listen and can hear what is read to them while still in the womb but also that this early reading helps to develop their language skills by helping to develop the areas of the brain that will be used later on to speak. After birth, a child should be read to at least once a day. The reading does not need to be long for it to have a great impact. This act of reading to a child not only helps to embed reading as a learned behavior but also helps the reader (the parent) and the child bond more closely. Emotions are shared and learned through stories and lessons about life are passed on also through the drama of the stories that are read.

In truth, as an African people, this sharing of stories was always a significant part of our development as a people, especially as children. Instead of books, the village elders and

---

[2] *www.earlyliteracylearning.org/cellreviews/cellreviews_v5_n4.pdf*

[3] *http://jslhr.pubs.asha.org/article.aspx?articleid=2212310*

visiting *griots* (story tellers) would recall stories and parables to the community and within families which would in turn serve the functions that reading does today. As a child becomes older, they should be made to try to tell stories from what they see in books. The adult can read alongside them to deliver the full story. During the early years of a child's life, the child should be helped in their literacy by being taught key early sight words by memory and later by sounding out. If the parent is bilingual, the child should be encouraged to speak, read AND write both languages. This will not only help them to have a wider information source later on in their teen and adult life but also help their brain to develop a whole set of complex pathways that they would not use if they spoke only one language, especially English. English does not use a full range of tonal and guttural sounds as some other languages especially those from the African continent. Hence why it is difficult for those of us who only speak English to not only learn other languages but also to even pronounce names of those derived from other languages.

As the child leaves the toddler years and begins to develop independent reading skills, they should spend at least 15 - 30 minutes a day reading on their own. Following this independent reading period, parents should ask the child to recall what they read and question them on some key events or characters in the stories. As the child's vocabulary and reading ability improves, the level of difficulty of books should also increase but being sure that the books provided are accessible to the child and of interest. Reading material need not be limited to formal reading books or novels, etc. but can also take the form of informative magazines such as National Geographic or other hobby-based publications. This enforced and encouraged reading time should not decrease as the child enters their teenage years. In fact, this period becomes an even more critical time for a child to be encouraged and given time to read independently without any other distractions such as a television or game console. The reading will not only continue to enhance the child's overall literacy including vocabulary, spelling and grammar but also the child's knowledge of the world around them. This then will have a direct impact on the child's academics as well as their ability to interact and communicate with others, especially those outside of their immediate social circles. With all of this in mind, by the time a child reaches young adulthood, a lifelong love of reading will have been embedded which will be an invaluable tool for them to navigate the waters of their life going forward.

Similar to reading, developing early numeracy will help set the foundation for the ability of a child to use numbers to communicate and analyze their world in their adult life. This has a direct impact on what career paths may be accessible to them, how they can manage their finances and other aspects of their home lives and how they relate to changes around them in the world such as the fluctuations of the local and global economy. Not only that, but mathematics along with observation and logic form the basis of scientific understanding and with a strong mathematical foundation, many mysteries of life can be uncovered.

Research shows that the foundations for later understanding of mathematics occurs before a child enters mainstream schooling with other children.[4] This means that it is the home and the child's parents that provide the early introduction and

---

[4] *www.child-encyclopedia.com/numeracy/according-experts/early-predictors-mathematics-achievement-and-mathematics-learning*

understanding to numeracy that is later built on in school. The research shows that rather than just the recognition of numbers as characters being important, it is the ability of the child to recognize numbers as symbols representing sets of objects that is critical. Parents can do this by speaking to children in terms of numbers and objects during their playtime with them. Playing with children is critical to them developing both early literacy and numeracy. Very young children should be provided with toys in which patterns of number sets can be seen both directly and indirectly. An abacus is a great teaching tool and young children always find them interesting. Blocks for building and toys that involve building and putting pieces together are also excellent at helping the brain develop pathways relating to recognizing patterns.

Counting with children as young as possible and into the toddler stage also helps develop number recognition. My mother used to count the toes on my feet and then tickle me at number 10! This common play action between mother and child actually then teaches the child about 10 as a discrete number set from early ages. Children love to count, and they should be encouraged to count to 10, then 20, then 50 and then 100 when they can. Playing games that involve counting and count-downs like hide and seek are great tools for this. As they get into the toddler years, a child should spend about 15-30 minutes two to three times a week learning about numbers and number patterns. The pace that numeracy and literacy is taught in schools is too slow for our brilliant boys and girls of African-descent and so parents should not feel limited by the content that the child's school is delivering. Putting up posters and information sheets that relate to numeracy and literacy in a learning area will be a great help and this area can be used as a learning zone for children independently and with parents. Once children can count to 10 and recognize numbers, parents should introduce them to concepts such as adding and subtracting. Teach them to use their fingers or objects such as blocks or coins to add or subtract. Once these concepts are understood, they can be introduced to using numbers as symbols to add or subtract, which should also then be linked to the same process by using number sets. From there, children can then be taught about dividing and fractions by using these same number sets of objects. (i.e. half of 10 blocks is 5, etc.). Learning about measurement and having opportunities and tools to measure things is critical. Allow children to play with tape measures and rulers and encourage them to measure parts of their body and the objects they see around them. Opportunities to apply all of these numeracy concepts should be sought when out and about – for example, rows in a garden or items on a shelf or animals in a field, etc. - math is everywhere! This understanding of patterns within number sets can then be extended to early aspects of geometry and the mathematics of shapes such as symmetry and repeating patterns.

Music is also a great tool that is directly linked to numeracy. Singing and playing an instrument directly involves the phenomenon of rhythm, frequency and harmony. Teaching and getting children from young ages to play instruments such as drums, pianos, etc. will develop areas of their brain that not only are responsible for creativity but also those that are responsible for recognizing patterns. As they become even more advanced in their mathematical understanding, it is then helpful to relate more abstract concepts of mathematics to children. In upper primary, they can be introduced to working with numbers by representing them as non-numeric symbols - i.e. early foundations for algebra. By this time, the child will be encountering a robust range of mathematical information at school and the parent can help the child by working with them through areas of their subjects that they find challenging as well as insisting that they spend independent learning time on mathematics at regular intervals each week with resources provided.

Once in upper primary and teenage years, parents of children from an African-descent should be sure to ground their child's base knowledge with the wisdom that Africans have employed mathematics for 1000s of years and provide them with examples of this. Good examples are the still used theories of Pythagoras today who was known to have studied in ancient Egypt, the astronomy and astrological relationships between the pyramids and the stars, the ancient calendar systems present in ancient societies such as the 'Adam's Calendar' site in South Africa, etc. Likewise, they should challenge the child to interpret the world using mathematics in everyday activities and observances such as patterns in nature, observations of machinery and how they work (i.e. gears on a bike, wheels on a car, etc.) and of course most importantly, concepts of time and space (clocks, maps, measurement and distance, etc.). Finally, learning about mathematical subjects such as percentages, interests and depreciation as it relates to money will also be critical to that child acquiring wealth and financial stability in their adult years, something that is addressed in the next chapter.

Principle 3

Financial Literacy and Wealth Building - It's only through building individual and family wealth that the those of African-descent can truly become powerful as a collective people.

THERE SEEMS TO be many quotes that speak negatively about the influence of money on people. We have all heard them! Quotes like 'the love of money is the root of all evil' and 'money can't buy you happiness'. There are nuggets of wisdom in these sayings of course but they do not tell the whole story. Let's take the first saying - 'the love of money is the root of all evil'. For those who research the quote, they will know that the original source of the saying is a biblical one (1 Timothy 6:10). While the saying does refer to love of money being a corrupting influence, it's the verses before that provide the context. What the author is trying to convey is that a desire for money that is received through ill-gotten or immoral gains is not a positive thing and that those whose hunger for material things is so great that they will stoop to these methods to

obtain it will not have a beneficial outcome either for themselves as individuals or their community. Unfortunately, this
corrupting influence on the black community due to a lust
for money and material things is all too clear to see for any
observer. Many of our communities are plagued by the self-
genocidal acts of drug sales and violent crime perpetuated
towards our own people, allowing a select few to gain mon-
etarily but with the resulting negative impacts on individuals
and families being devastating.

Similarly, the second saying that 'money can't buy happiness' needs to be taken in context. We all know too well that
having access to large amounts of money and being wealthy
is no guarantee to being happy in life. How many millionaires
and well-paid businessmen and celebrities have taken their
lives due to emotional distress despite not having a material want in the world. A research study found that in some
cases those who were more wealthy were more likely to commit suicide than those who were poorer, perhaps because of
a hesitance to admit their problems before receiving help.[5]
However, in these cases, it is not the money that may be caus-
ing the unhappiness that the people have in their lives but
rather underlying psychological, emotional or mental health
issues that they have not been able to cope with.

Despite both of these sayings having kernels of truth
that of course should be reflected on and heeded to, only
a fool would suggest that access to money and having control over one's finances is not important to both individuals
and communities. In order to understand why understanding money and finance may be important to our black boys,

---

[5] *http://news.bbc.co.uk/1/hi/health/1160222.stm*

perhaps we need to speak about what money actually is first. Money is a word used to denote a mechanism of exchange for goods and services. While we have become used to seeing money as the paper currency that we exchange on a regular basis, money does not have to take this form. In ancient times, commodities like salt was used as a currency of exchange and symbolic items such as cowrie shells have also filled this role. Precious metals have been important materials for representing wealth and have been used as a method of exchange since ancient times. With this in mind, it can be clearly seen that it is not really the money as a physical object that is important, it is the representation of wealth that the various forms represent. Knowing what the term *'wealth'* refers to is critically important for a young boy to understand from an early age. In my view, wealth refers to the total sum of not only money but anything that is of exchangeable value that one has, specifically regarding material possessions or resources.

Financial literacy then is having competence in what money and wealth is and how to manage them effectively in their various forms. The ultimate aim for building this financial literacy in our young boys is to help them to build individual wealth which can then promote familial and community wealth. Wealth is only truly powerful when it is inter-generational. Inter-generational wealth allows not only the members of a family to be materially sound and have their needs met but also generations of offspring that are still yet to be born. In this way, these future generations can maintain the value systems and social structures that are set by their ancestors and not see them eroded. It is no coincidence that the prevailing value system that most people in the western world live under are those of western European origin. This is a simple result of cause and effect.

It is western European families and family lines that have acquired the highest amounts of wealth and so it is these people that run both businesses, economies and governments, all institutions in which their values systems can be transferred and promulgated throughout time. Global bank Credit Suisse reports that the majority of the world's wealth is owned by only 1% of the total population and, of this 1%, most of it is concentrated in the hands of Europe's elite as a collective block.[6] On the flip side of this, the poorest countries are in Africa and, in the major Western nations, the poorest people as a block are those of ethnic minority communities. The US Census Bureau list blacks in America as the lowest in terms of income and the lowest rates in home ownership.

Reversing this trend has to start at the individual level and then be passed on to families which in turn will build strong communities and eventually a strong nation. So, what are the core principles that need to be introduced and passed on to our young boys of African-descent?

Step 1 - Toddler: Teach boys about the value of money

Teach boys from a young age the value of money, in particular, the value of managing and saving money. All children become fascinated with money once they learn that it can be used to get things of value. Foster this interest and early financial literacy by encouraging them to count and save any money they may get from relatives or from doing small chores around the

---

[6] *www.zerohedge.com/news/2013-06-02/its-1-world-who-owns-what-223-trillion-global-wealth*

house. Make sure they keep a physical object to hold their germinating savings so that they can better visualize the principles of accumulation.

Step 2 - 5 to 10 years: Engrain the principle of saving and accumulation

As children get older, provide them with a small allowance that they can use to save and manage. At this stage, children can be assisted to open an electronic bank account, preferably in a black-owned bank or credit union. Encourage them to treat this account as a savings account that is untouchable. Engrain in them the principles of the extreme wealthy like Warren Buffet who says, "Do not save what is left after spending, but spend what is left after saving."

Step 3 - 10 to teenage years: Work hard to cancel out the western media's onslaught of materialism brainwashing

Beyond 10 years of age, children become hyper-conscious of themselves as individuals and how they compare to the other peers around them. Part of this is an examination of the material possessions that they have and that their peers have. Western media, backed by big business, sees children as a market to exploit. The idea that happiness can be purchased by buying things is constantly rammed down children's throats through every medium of advertising you can think of - radio, music, television and cinema to name a few. This onslaught of advertising is especially accelerated around and during so-called holiday periods such as Christmas and Halloween. Families literally will go broke over these times of the year purchasing valueless items such as toys for their children, only to see these same items discarded with a few weeks if not days after they are received. This materialism is one of the key things that leads to our impoverishment as a community - as the saying goes "rich people stay rich by living like they are broke while broke people stay broke by living like they are rich". Children should be taught this axiom above all else and be given the truth about the economic state of our ethnic community, what keeps people of African-descent in this state of perpetual impoverishment and what needs to be done in order to change this paradigm.

Step 4 - Teenage years to adult life: Pay yourself first with your earnings by saving at least 10% of your income

The fact of the matter is that most of us are not taught principles towards financial literacy and wealth building. Many of us unfortunately learn only after trial and error and, sadly, even financial crises. Imagine if we employed this principle from the first time we started earning a formal salary. Look at some simple math - if $100 was saved every month from the age of 20 to the age of 30, a ten-year period, that individual would have $12,000 in savings at the end. If $200, the savings would double to $24,000. Suppose the time period was also doubled - this would be a whopping $48,000 in savings after 20 years - that is, by the time the individual is 40 years old. How many of us can say we have $48,000 in savings when we were or will be 40 years old! And these sums do not factor in the benefits of interest, compounding and potential investments. Paying yourself first by placing 10% of your earnings into savings should take place before any other bills are paid, no matter what you owe and to who!

Step 5 - Adult life: Invest part of your savings into a diverse portfolio of both passive income and long-term secure investment vehicles

If savings are the foundation of wealth, investment is the bricks and mortar that builds your financial house. Passive income is income that is earned by investing in mechanisms that produce further income without further or substantial work. Examples of passive income would be things like royalties from sales of a product that you have created and wholesale to retailers, holding a license on a particular product or service that people pay for to use or having an advertising tool on a website that you make a fee from when people utilize that product or service. However, the best tool of passive income by far is the possession of real estate. As stated earlier, blacks as an ethnic group have some of the lowest home ownership rates around the world. This lack of home ownership affects our family stability and thus disrupts black people from having secure access to housing from which to build wealth from. Lack of home ownership also affects our ability to earn passive income through income sources like renting. There have been clear increases in the cost of renting over the past century and although house prices have also increased, this trend alone shows that rental income is an excellent source of passive income.

A wealth portfolio is strongest when it is diverse and looks to take care of both near term cash liquidity as well as longer term considerations regarding wealth acquisition. In this regard, investing in long-term secure investment vehicles such as precious metals and commodities can be valuable. Any investor in stocks will tell you that it is a risky business however, precious metals like gold and silver have stood the test of time as a safe and secure investment. Remember, long term secure investment vehicles like gold are not those that should be looked at as a potential source of liquid cash in the near term. Instead, these investments are what can be termed generational investments and they are those, like property, that can be passed onto your children who then can pass them onto their children, etc. Like property, gold appreciates and not depreciates so its value will be greatest as a sum of the change in value over long periods of time. So, if gold cannot or rather should not be used as a source of liquid cash, how is it useful to those in the present? This is when we need to understand the principles of equity value and realize that liquid money can be loaned based off the collateral value in an owned equity. So, if a present generation has ownership of valuable gold assets for example, these assets can then be used as a guarantee for forms of credit to fund other endeavors that might in turn generate passive income or entrepreneurial opportunities that might be riskier.

While teaching these principles of financial literacy over the course of a young boy of African-descent formative years is vitally important, it cannot be over-emphasized how critical it also is to embed knowledge of the rich history of wealth that they descend from as African people. Efforts should be made to teach them the history of great and wealthy nations like that of the dynasties of Kemet (Egypt) and those of Mali including Mansa Musa purported to be the world's richest man in history as well as more modern-day success stories of wealth such as Madame CJ Walker, S.B. Fuller, Jay-Z and Oprah Winfrey. Efforts should be made to ensure that the examples shared with them come from both men and women of African-descent as well as from a diverse range of industries or entrepreneurial areas, not just those the media likes to highlight such as entertainment and music.

This historical grounding is crucial in establishing a mind-set in our boys that recognizes success and wealth as their birth right rather than as some unachievable, fantastical status that they can never obtain. Society and the media work hard to make it seem that being wealthy is something only normal for an elite few, so that means us as parents need to work even harder to ensure that this misconception is not the reality in the minds of our boys of African-descent.

Principle 4

Knowledge of Geography, History and Culture - "A people without the knowledge of their history, origin and culture is like a tree without roots."

THE FAMOUS QUOTE by Marcus Garvey above is well known by many but what is the deeper meaning of this oft repeated saying by this great sage and freedom fighter for the African race. A good starting point is to focus on the part of the phrase which reads *'like a tree without roots'*. Anyone with even a basic understanding in biology will know that the roots of a tree serve two important functions - stability and absorption of water and minerals. Simply put, a tree without roots could never survive. For one, it would not have the necessary stability to stand tall and take in the life-giving light it needs to photosynthesize to make food for its cells. Secondly, without the absorption the roots provide, the tree would eventually dry out due to a lack of water and its cells would become dysfunctional as a result of not having the necessary water and minerals they need to carry out their vital functions. With this in mind, Marcus Garvey was making it clear that similar to a tree without roots, a people without knowledge of their history, origin and culture would suffer the same fate - eventual death.

Although this quote by Marcus Garvey is one of the most well known to many, he had many more that can help us to understand what the importance and relevance of Principle Four really is. Marcus is quoted as saying "History is the land-mark by which we are directed into the true course of life. The history of a movement, the history of a nation, the history of a race is the guide-post of that movement's destiny, that nation's destiny, that race's destiny. What you do today that is worthwhile, inspires others to act at some future time."[7] it is history that affords stability and direction to a people. This is also embodied in the west African principle of *'sankofa'* - which is to say, *"go back and get it"*. Marcus Garvey gives a clear message to us collectively - what we do today will affect the actions of others in the future. Likewise, what has been done in the past has affected our actions today. Without hav-ing knowledge of their history, the good and the bad, our young boys of African-descent will not be able to effectively understand how we arrived in the position we are in today as a people and more importantly, how their actions can influence where our people's destiny may lie in the future.

And culture? What is its importance? Culture refers to "the way of life, especially the general customs and beliefs,

---

[7] *Garvey, Marcus, 1887-1940. Philosophy and Opinions of Marcus Garvey / Edited by Amy Jacques-Garvey; with a New Pref. by Hollis R. Lynch. New York: Atheneum, 1969., pg. 4*

of a particular group of people at a particular time".[8] For many people around the world, whether we like it or not, black people have certain cultures (i.e. general customs and beliefs) associated with them in this present day and many of these cultural attributes, especially for those concerning our young people are not positive. Young black culture can be associated with degrading music and imagery to both males and females, lifestyles involving a focus on drugs and gangs and relationships characterized by single mothers and deadbeat dads. For a young boy growing up in today's world full of the imagery channeled into their mind by the media, the cultural framework that can be used to provide the stability and direction they need can be fraught with danger. But was this cultural expression attributed to our people always so? Definitely not!

Marcus Garvey's words can also help us here. He says "This race of ours gave civilization, gave art, gave science; gave literature to the world. But it has been the way with races and nations. The one race stands out prominently in the one century or in the one age; and in another century or age it passes off the stage of action, and another race takes its place. The Negro once occupied a high position in the world, scientifically, artistically and commercially, but in the balancing of the great scale of evolution, we lost our place and someone, other than ourselves occupies the stand we once held." This is the message that must be taught to our young boys. Not only do they need to have knowledge of their history so they can understand how and where their destiny should lie but also, they need to truly understand the significance that African culture played in shaping the world they live in today so that

---

[8] *http://dictionary.cambridge.org/dictionary/english/group*

they have a counter-balance to the negative imagery projected to them on a daily basis. In the words of Marcus again, "Education is the medium by which a people are prepared for the creation of their own particular civilization, and the advancement and glory of their own race." But what should we make sure our young black boys are taught so that they can once again seek to occupy a high place within the civilized nations of the world?

Geography

Of utmost importance is geography. Without geography, the dates and facts of history have no real context. Both physical geography and political geography are important. Physical geography will provide an orientation to a child's understanding of his spatial position on this planet relative to other physical landmarks. Political geography will give the child an understanding of how the socio-political landscape of the societies of the world have changed and continue to change. The following core issues should be shared with our boys:

1. Maps lie...

Maps don't really lie but the pictures they present can be deceptive! It is important a child understands that the projection of a map will distort the size and position of the objects on it. This is particularly important regarding understanding where their ancestors came from - the continent of Africa, its true position and how big it really is in context to the other parts of the world. The map below shows a true projection of Africa in relation to the other so-called continents and its true massive size can be fully appreciated.

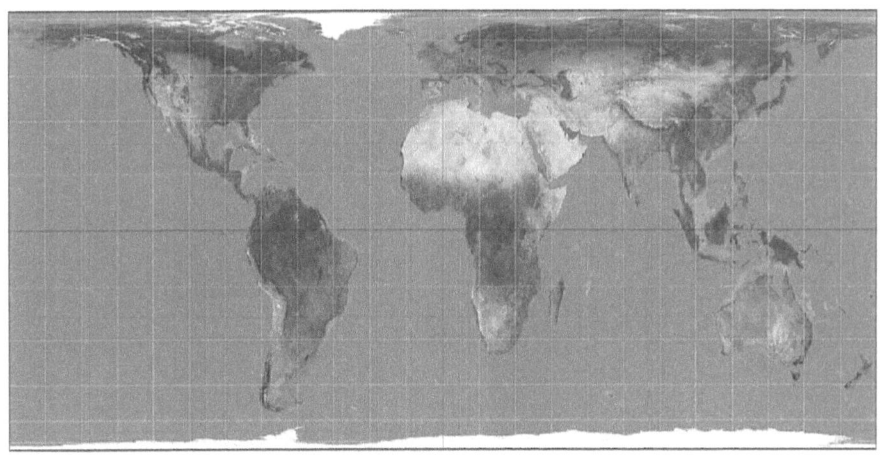

Hobo-Dyer Map Projection[9]

2. Political borders are not real...

Well, again, the borders are real, politically speaking that is, but they constantly change, especially when the eons of time are considered. In particular, the political borders that now make up Africa into hundreds of countries were not always so and more importantly, were put in place as a result of colonialism by western imperial powers only in the 20th centuries who sought to control and exploit the human and natural resources of our people for themselves.

3. People of African-descent exist and live all around the Earth!

Literally! Too often, young people have a poor understanding of how diverse and widespread people of African-descent are throughout the world. J.A. rogers in his book *Sex and Race:*

---

[9] *https://commons.wikimedia.org/wiki/File:Hobo%E2%80%93Dyer_ projection_SW.jpg / Author: Strebe [Accessed 14/06/2019]*

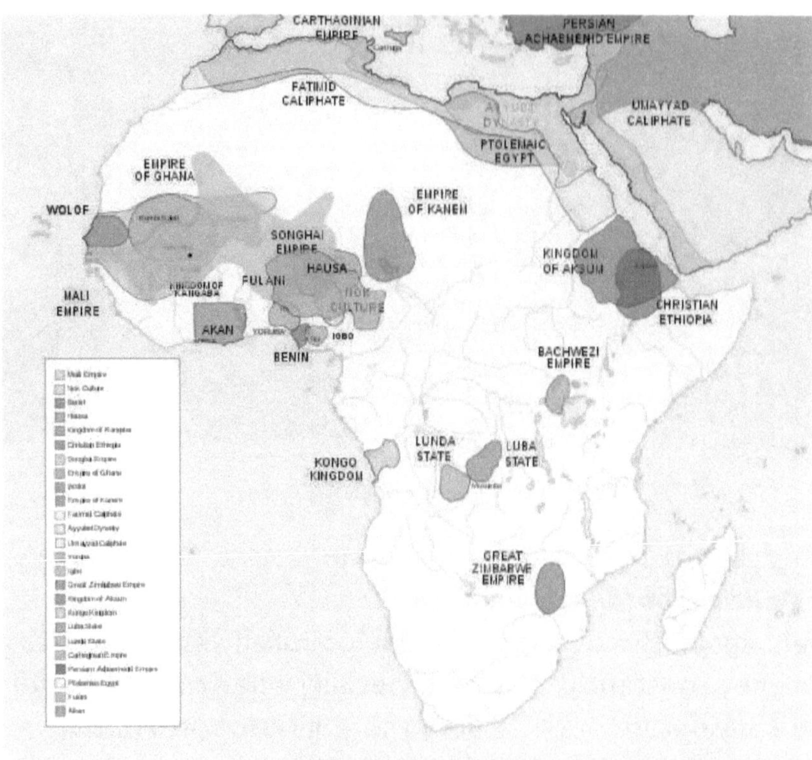

Artistic impressionist diachronic map showing pre-colonial cultures of Africa (~ 500 BCE to 1500 CE)[10]

Negro-Caucasian Mixing in All Ages and All Lands[11] as well as intrepid ethno-archaeologist and author Runoko Rashidi in his many published works show how black people can be found around the world and on all continents. Despite this diversity

---

[10] *https://commons.wikimedia.org/wiki/File:African-civilizations-map-pre-colonial.svg [Accessed: 14/06/2019] / Author: Jeff Israel (ZyMOS))*

[11] *Rogers, J. A., author. Sex and Race. Volume 1, The Old World: Negro-Caucasian Mixing in All Ages and All Lands. St. Petersburg, Florida: Helga M. Rogers, 1968.*

in existence of black people around the world, genetic studies have and continue to find the same pattern - their origin of all mankind are from the original people of the African continent!

<u>History and Culture</u>

History and culture are intertwined for as a people express themselves and develop their culture, history records this change. Our young boys of African-descent need counter images to those that they are presented with today as examples of who they can and should be. As Marcus Garvey pointed out, African people have a long history of high culture and have contributed much to the world and its development over history. It's important that our young boys understand and know this and see actual real life, concrete examples for them to reflect their own existence on.

Key historical icons of African peoples are many but there are some of greater historical significance than others. African people are the most ancient on Earth and sharing with a child the diversity of these ancient African societies is a good starting point in enriching their historical framework. In particular, the ancient cultures of Cush (Ethiopia), Kemet (Egypt), Nubia (Sudan), Songhai and Mali, the Olmec, the Moors and the ancient Dravidians are some of the most powerful nations to have ever existed on our planet and all were made up of African peoples. Children should be made to read and study the culture of these nations, focusing on their geographical location and cultural developments as it relates to contributions to society today. There they will find that the very foundations of religion, science and politics that are society is built on in present times has evolved from much of these ancient cultures. This book is too limited to go into the details of all the rich history and cultures of these societies but there are many excellent reference sources written by black authors on these nations and many more.

Here is my list of top 10 recommended books for parents to read so that they can be well equipped to share the wonderful history of their ancestors with their children.

1. They Came Before Columbus - Ivan Van Sertima
2. Wonderful Ethiopians of the Cushite empire Houston, Drusilla Dunjee
3. Sundiata, D.T. Niane
4. African Presence in Early Asia, Runoko Rashidi
5. Black Man of the Nile, Yosef Ben-Jochannan
6. African Origins of Major "Western Religions", Yosef Ben-Jochannan
7. Civilization or Barbarism: An Authentic Anthropology, Chiekh Anta Diop
8. The African Origin of Civilization: Myth or Reality, Chiekh Anta Diop
9. The Interesting Narrative of the Life of Olaudah Equiano
10. Nile Valley Contributions to Civilization, Anthony Browder

Although the education of our young black boys through sharing with them examples of the high culture of our ancestors is important, it is also important for them to be grounded in history and culture that is closer to home geographically and chronologically also. The history of how black people came to be dispersed from the African continent is critical to share and our young boys of African-descent need to understand where their direct ancestors came from, what their culture was like there and how it differs from that attributed to black culture today. In particular, they should be taught about the history of the global slave trade in Africa, both the trans-Atlantic and the trans-Pacific, which is not talked about as much. They should be provided with real figures on the numbers of Africans thought to have been taken from the continent, the areas where they came from, how they were transported, to where and most importantly, by whom. These discussions can then be followed up by information on colonialism and how European powers divided up Africa into many of the political entities that we still see existing there today.

Books like *How Europe Underdeveloped Africa* by Walter Rodney can be key sources of vital facts. Information should be given on the customs and practices of the African people that their ancestors most likely descended from. Genetic research through DNA testing can be employed to help make these discussions more real to them as well as the creation of a family tree that goes as far back as possible. The customs of contemporary traditional African peoples should be shared such as those of West Africa like the Ashanti and Twi, South Africa like the Zulu, East Africa like the Maasai and North Africa like the Bedouin and original black Arabs.

Finally, the modern-day traditions and cultures of the black societies and family practices that our black boys come from should also be discussed with them and exemplified with a sense of pride. Although our ancestors were taken from Africa much of their culture and traditional practices can still be found in our modern-day way of living. For example, in the island of Bermuda where I am from, we have a tradition called the 'Gombey' which are groups of masquerade (masked and costumed) dancers that wear bright and colorful clothing in a specific style and that dance to a specific drum beat. This same tradition can be found throughout other parts of the Caribbean and has its origin in the cultures of West Africa. In fact, the word 'gombey' is thought to mean 'drum' and is similar to the west African word for a specific type of drum called 'djembe'. The Caribbean holds countless other examples of the remnants of our African culture - from the remaining of traditional African words in the modern creole dialects spoken in places like Jamaica and Cuba, to foods and dishes that are almost identically prepared to those in Africa. In the US, the African influence is seen strongly in the carnival traditions of New Orleans and the traditions of the Gullah Geechee of the south east coast of the United States. No matter where you are from, as Peter Tosh sang 'as long as you are a black man, you are an African' and finding some aspect of African identity in your modern history and culture of your family and country of origin will not be hard.

Gombey of Bermuda[12]

[12] www.flickr.com/photos/127744844@N06/36468325925 [Accessed 14/6/2019]

Masquerade Dancers of St. Kitts[13]

Finally, if time and expenses allow, visiting as many sites of historical importance in relation to African history and culture as possible with our young boys of African-descent. These can be as simple as visits to the elderly in the family who can share with them their experiences that they went through in their lifetime or more elaborate ones such as visits to important historical landmarks. It is especially powerful and rewarding for young people to visit places of power where their ancestors' spirits will still remain such as the various slave castles that were used to hold slaves during the slave trade. Regale the stories of what happened in these locations and let our young boys feel their warrior spirit arise within them.

---

[13] www.flickr.com/photos/prayitnophotography/28899130408 [Accessed 14/6/2019]

Principle 5

Fitness and Health - A warrior must be both mentally and physically strong; to be a king now you need add only wisdom.

ONE OF THE most damaging aspects of the legacy of the trans-oceanic slave trade in Africans has been the loss of the diverse spectrum of rites of passage rituals that would have helped to transition our young boys onto their journey towards being young men. A rite of passage ritual usually takes the form of a specific set of traditional practices that a person must undertake at key milestones in their life. Both male and females in African traditional societies are expected to undertake various types of rites of passage during their lifetime. For example, the Maasai of Kenya have a rite of passage for boys at the age of puberty in which they are circumcised and thereby initiated into the warrior clan of their particular tribe. This rite of passage is led by the elders of the village who themselves have gone through this initiation ceremony themselves and thus have the wisdom and knowledge to share their experiences with the young boys as to what it takes and means to become a warrior. The boys prepare themselves through fasting and separation from their families and in this way the rite of passage influences the boys' physical and mental character.

Likewise, the Hamar people of Ethiopia also hold a coming of age rite of passage for young men in their tribal community. The penultimate challenge during this rite is to jump on and run over the backs of several cattle. The cattle, which include both male and female, are said to represent the various sectors of the Hamar community - males, females and children. The backs of the cattle are smeared with dung and mud and are very slippery. The young men must run over the backs of the cattle four times and if successful, they will be initiated into the Maza (manhood) class of the society and are now eligible to marry, have children and most importantly, own their own cattle! To not be able to complete the challenge is considered a shameful event amongst the Hamar and because of this the young men put great thought and effort into being able to complete this task. To not do so would be to bring great dishonor to themselves and their families.

Unfortunately, for Africans now in the diaspora and even those on the continent living in modern non-traditional society settings, much of the rite of passage systems has been forgotten. And while the specific physical rituals that accompanied the various rites of passage systems are amongst those vital components no longer remembered, what is even more significant is the absence of the psychological and character-building effect that these rites of passage events had on our young boys that would lead to further physical and mental development. To pass the many rites of passage rituals of yesteryear, a boy knew that they had to be both mentally and physically fit. Luckily, due to the lifestyle of the boys resulting from the living conditions they would grow up in, both mental and physical fitness was not hard to come by. The demands on boys in rural societies are much more physically demanding than most of what children living in today's urban and sub-urban societies face. Rather than sitting on couches playing video games and watching hours of television, boys growing up in the Maasai, the Hamar and other traditional rural-based African tribal groups would have to tend cattle, fetch water and collect firewood. To work was to survive and to not work was to starve and, in some cases, die.

But what of our boys today? The Government Office for Science reports that global obesity rates for children are on the rise and, in particular, those that are leading this increase are in the developed nations the world.[14] Along with this trend in rising obesity has come rising numbers of children and adults suffering from type-2 diabetes and other lifestyle related diseases such as heart disease and cancer. More and more children are becoming inactive[15] and this inactivity is fueling the rise in obesity amongst young people. Again, children in developed nations are leading the way in this negative trend (see chart below[16]).

This lack of activity not only affects a child's health but also a child's mentality too. Activity means that the body is being tested in some way and is being forced to make decisions. In making decisions, the brain has to problem solve and new pathways are formed in order to allow it to do so.

---

[14] http://news.bbc.co.uk/1/hi/health/7151813.stm

[15] http://www.phitworld.org/News_Archive/EYE_OPENING__
Activity_vs_Calories.htm

[16] https://www.bbc.co.uk/news/health-25576400

Percentage of overweight and obese adults with BMI greater than 25, by region

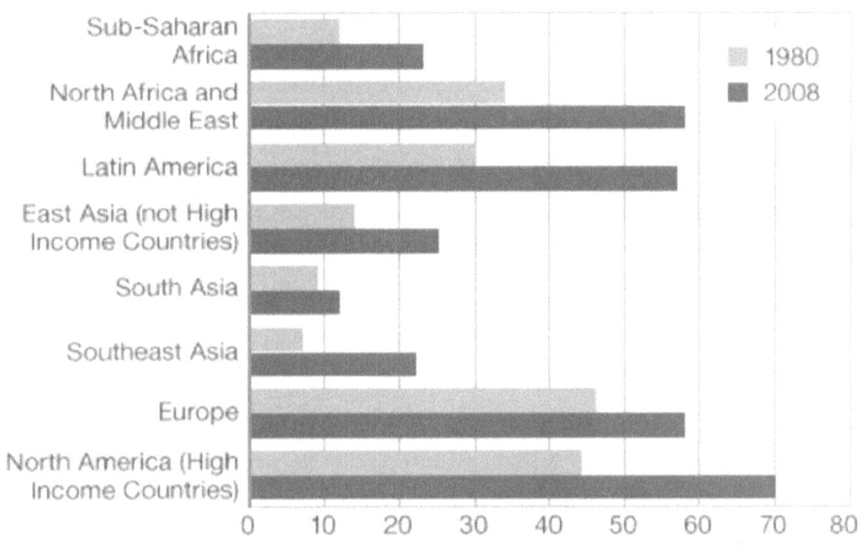

Source: Overseas Development Institute

Something as simple as running involves hundreds or even thousands of calculations being done by your brain every second. With more complex activities such as organized sports, both those solo and team-based, those complex thought and decision-making processes are even more numerous. This in turn improves the ABCs (agility, balance and coordination) capabilities of the body which in turn allows more complex and subtle physical tasks to be completed. Secondly, when active, the body needs to take in much more oxygen and this extra oxygen enriches the blood and cells in this life-giving element. Activity improves circulation, as the heart, which is a muscle, beats faster and becomes stronger and blood is carried to the extremities of the body more efficiently, including the brain. Thus, a person that exercises will think more clearly and be more alert. Exercise in the outdoors means exposure to nature and the natural environment which has a proven calming effect on the mind. Children that exercise tend to be more emotionally balanced, calm and relaxed.[17]

With all this in mind, and with the lack of formal rites of passage systems for our boys in many of today's modern societies, it is imperative that we facilitate and encourage our young boys to exercise and be physically fit. There is no way that we can expect our young black boys to take on the responsibilities of being men in our communities and to carry out these responsibilities such as to serve and protect the members of their community as warriors and later on as elders, if they do not have a holistic state of fitness fostered at a young age. This attention to having a mentally and physically fit body should start as young as possible and the toddler stage is a good time.

Steps towards developing Physical Fitness over a Young Boys Lifetime
Step 1 - Emphasize physical activity, health and fitness from a young age.

Parents should talk to their child about being healthy and physically fit from a young age. As was covered in Principle 1 on nutrition, the primary factor in determining good physical health is through what we eat. Children should not only be provided with healthy, nutritious food options but also educated and encouraged to make positive choices regarding foods when they become more independent. Parents should also emphasize to children the importance of exercise and being

---

[17] www.apa.org/monitor/2011/12/exercise.aspx

active regarding being physically fit. From the early toddler stage, parents should play with their children in active ways and encourage them to go outside to play or to participate in a sport of some sort. There are so many excellent sports programs now for young children that are based on fun and learning.

Step 2 - Parents need to model positive examples of being physically fit.

If Step 1 above can be considered 'talk the talk', Step 2 here is 'walk the walk'. Children should see their parents participating in activities towards developing good physical fitness so that they can observe the beneficial effects of their participation as well as have a model for what they can work towards. Fathers in particular need to be a good role model to their young boys regarding being active. This activity can take multiple forms - working out, sports, martial arts, hobbies such as cycling, karting or other forms of leisure such as gardening, etc. The list is endless. We cannot expect our children to become involved in things we are not.

Step 3 - Parents should be physically active and exercise with their children.

One of the most enjoyable things my children love to do is climb trees with me! Often, I am up the tree before they are! I also made a point to work with my children in any sports that they took up - not just encourage them to practice but made time to go out and practice with them. From a young age, whenever the opportunity presented itself, I would encourage my children to participate in the exercise or activity I was doing. Whether it was early morning running for the older children, gardening with the whole family or encouraging my toddler to stretch with me during a home yoga session.

Step 4 - Provide children with the tools and experiences needed to stay physically fit.

I have to give maximum respect to my mother as she made sure that if I showed an interest in a particular activity, she would find a way to get me involved. I have had a wide range of interests over my young life ranging from track and field, horseback riding, skateboarding, SCUBA diving, martial arts (Kung Fu and Wing Chun) to football (soccer). Thankfully, my mother somehow found a way to provide an opportunity for me to participate in these interests and many I still do to this day when I can. Of course, some activities may be expensive, but it takes just a little thought to involve children in physical activities that are both fun and healthy. Every child should have a bike to ride, a ball to kick or throw and an eager parent to take them to the nearest public play or sports ground to get active in.

Step 5 - Encourage children to put down the computer devices, turn off the television and go outside NO MATTER THE WEATHER!

There seems to be a self-imposed restriction on many people of African-descent enjoying the outdoors if the temperature is cold or the weather is rainy. I am often dismayed when I would take my young children to the playground when living in England only for us to be the only black family around. If our children are not on the playground, where are they then? Of course, this is a generalization but nevertheless the point is critical. Our children need to be encouraged to spend more time outside and not cooped up indoors as it is not healthy. Being indoors encourages a sedentary lifestyle and this can promote all sorts of negative impacts on health - like poor circulation, poor flexibility and weight gain. Additionally, the indoor air quality of many homes is very poor when compared to that outdoors, especially in regard to the oxygen/carbon dioxide balance and other indoor contaminants such as dust and volatile organic compounds from synthetic materials. In today's increasingly commercialized world, electronic devices are heavily marketed to children and can easily become a source of excessive attention and almost obsessive behaviors at time. Playing electronic games and watching tv excessively has been proven in research to be directly linked to negative effects on social and emotional development not to mention posture and hand-eye coordination.[18]

Step 6 - Transition young teens into a warrior mentality as they head into adult life

If the toddler and primary school age of a young black boy's life is the preparation stage for a lifetime of physical fitness, it is at the teenage stage that preparation should become full-fledged boot camp. Our teenage black boys need to physically fit and able to stand up as strong warriors for the black community and serve the needs of its members, especially the most vulnerable - the elderly and the youth. Every teenage boy should be involved in some form of organized physical activity whether that be a sport, martial arts or other hobby. Teenage boys should also be encouraged to work out

---

[18] https://www.studenthealth.gov.hk/english/internet/report/files/e_report_wa.pdf

regularly (at least 2-3 times a week) and something as simple as doing 10 to 20 push-ups a day will go a long way to improving and strengthening their physique. Regular running is also an excellent way to open up the lungs of our boys so that they can breathe better and intake more oxygen into their body, especially in regard to its necessity to having a clear head for decision-making. Stretching and deep breathing should also be a key part of a weekly physical fitness routine. If this stretching and deep breathing is rooted in some aspect of inner spirituality such as Kemetic yoga, Tai Chi or Chi Gung, then the beneficial effect on both mind and body will be even more pronounced.

Step 7 - Sleep reinforces any health-giving efforts that we place on our body during waking hours.
Again, electronic devices are often a culprit here and many of our children (and adults) are not getting adequate amounts of sleep. Electronic devices radiate a specific range of wavelengths on the visible spectrum of light and of particular concern is those colors emitted in the blue light range. Research has shown that this range of light can significantly affect sleep patterns by disrupting the natural sleep cycle of the body, as well as have a detrimental effect on vision and eye health also.[19]

Sleep is also extremely important in regard to the production of vital hormones such as melatonin. Melatonin is only produced by the body, specifically the pineal gland in the brain, when the body is in dark conditions and asleep. Blue

---

[19] https://www.health.harvard.edu/staying-healthy/blue-light-has-a-dark-side

light directly interferes with the release of melatonin as the body is confused as to whether it is night or day. Melatonin is a powerful antioxidant and anti-inflammatory hormone, and therefore sleep can have very powerful healing effects on the body. A lack of sleep can not only cause tiredness and fatigue during the day, resulting in a loss of performance, but also can result in premature aging and illness.

Principle 6

Media - Information can either be a tool of oppression or upliftment. It's the person who controls it that decides.

IN HIS BOOK *1984*, famous author George Orwell wrote "He who controls the past controls the future. He who controls the present controls the past." For those who have not read the book, 1984 is a novel set in a nation where everything is controlled by a very small minority elite. It is a satirical story based on the concept of *'Big Brother'*, that is, living in a state where everything is watched, controlled and ordered by an unseen oligarchy bent on total control of the very minutiae of its society members. For some of us in today's world, this dystopian concept may not seem too far off from the world we live in today. Our movements are constantly watched by CCTV cameras and our spending tracked electronically by the cashless purchases we make. Even the things we search on the internet can be linked back to us and monitored by governments who say that they do it to help secure the safety of its citizens. This so-called altruistic intent is the subject of a larger debate for another day.

Not only are we under constant scrutiny in today's modern world, we are also under constant information overload. This is acutely less debatable. The information at our fingertips has led to this age in time to be called the information age, with subjects and content that would have taken our fore parents possibly great expense, time and distance to access, we can now access with just the touch or swipe of a screen. While this significant access to information has obvious tremendous benefits, it also comes with real costs. One cost is that most of the world's public sources of information, the media, are owned and controlled by relatively few people. This means that the type, content and context of information shared can also be manipulated by a small select proportion of the world's population, particularly to serve whatever their specific special interests or objectives may be.

The second major concern with the access to media by children today would be the type of content our children are able to access and the type of people that they are able to encounter through these information sources. Not only are physical threats to their safety a serious concern regarding online personalities they may interact with but the potential for psychological harm and social threats such as identity theft and cyber bullying also count as real issues of concern. Cyber bullying is a relatively new term coined in the 21st century and the challenges all young people potentially can face with having such an open access to each other and the wider world around them through social media is a constant struggle for parents, teachers and others in society charged with ensuring their wellbeing.

For those of African-descent, what is not often thought about is how the information our children are accessing both from mainstream and social media relates to and impacts on the celebration, liberation and upliftment of the black nation. The now late great Master teacher Ishakamusa Barashango is quoted as saying "People ask me why do I talk about black issues so much? Why? Because every day I wake up and look in the mirror I see a black face looking back at me! What else am I supposed to talk about!" I write this to say that every day our black boys get up and get ready to go out into the world, this is the reality they will face. And this is also the reality that the world will face them with. However, most of the content our children will see and hear on the media will not reflect this experience and definitely not reflect the glory of the African race and look to promote its liberation and upliftment.

There are real world historical examples of where the media has been used as a weapon towards the oppression of the black community, with men of African-descent being specific targets. The United States Government *Counter Intelligence Program*, abbreviated to *COINTELPRO*, was a surveillance, infiltration and propaganda program specifically structured to disrupt pro-black organizations and movements in the 1950s-1970. Although the mechanisms of disruption deployed by the *COINTELPRO* program were multi-faceted, the use of propaganda and spreading of false information was a crucial technique in their arsenal of tactics employed to discredit some of the key leaders of black upliftment movements of that time as well as cast shade on the intent of the movements themselves. Social activist leaders like Dr Martin Luther King Jr, Malcolm X and organizations like the Black Panther Party and their leaders were all targeted by this program. A key method used by the COINTELPRO to discredit these key figures was the creation of negative imagery and media specifically designed to foster animosity towards specific groups within the black community like the Black Panther Party, specifically in this case, by painting the groups as militant, dangerous and aggressive.

Another key scenario to show the power of the media can be seen regarding the advertising of tobacco products for smoking and how the presence of advertising can influence the rates of people who take up smoking as a practice. The book "Growing up Tobacco Free: Preventing Nicotine Addiction in Children and Youths"[20] showed clear connections between the advertisement of smoking products such as tobacco and the uptake by people, in particular, teens. Conversely, the evidence presented in the book also shows the how the removal of tobacco advertising also leads to reductions in the rates of people who take up smoking. These findings have also been replicated and supported by a more recent study conducted in England[21] and many others can be found with further investigation in published peer-reviewed scientific journals. Studies like these which show the power of the media to influence behavior as well as how the past history of the media has been used as a social and psychological weapon to the black community clearly demonstrates why monitoring the role and the content of the media consumed by our young boys is extremely important.

What then can be done? Firstly, parents should ensure that their children are grounded in a firm and comprehensive knowledge of their Self (mind, body and spirit) as well as in their history and culture. This strong knowledge of Self,

---

[20] www.ncbi.nlm.nih.gov/books/NBK236761/

[21] http://onlinelibrary.wiley.com/doi/10.1111/add.12501/full

especially if grounded on a firm foundation of positive information regarding the history and culture of black people, will
act as a buffer to the overload of negative imagery that they
will encounter in the various forms of the media. Secondly,
parents should not necessarily seek to limit what their children watch but more importantly take an active role in dis-
cussing the things that they may watch. Parents should not
be afraid to challenge themes appearing in the media that
are counterproductive to their overall upliftment as a boy of
African-descent and to the upliftment and betterment of the
African nation. Rather than let discussions on any topics of
disagreement be based on emotion, instead parents should
counter non-productive understandings of our young boys
with reason and evidence from the real world. For example,
the attraction and influence of the materialistic lifestyle por-
trayed in the music industry and marketed heavily to young
people can be countered with discussions and evidence based
on what are the actual incomes of many of the artists they
sometimes idolize and who actually owns the majority of the
world's wealth.

Thirdly, parents should actively seek out positive information to engage, educate AND entertain their boys. Vacuums
always want to be filled and so not having any positive sources
of media and entertainment to turn to will lead inevitably to
those gaps being filled with negative sources. A big part of
this is exposing our boys to sources of information and education outside of the normal purview of what society promotes
for them. Rather than spending hours watching pointless
television shows or playing mind-numbing video games, they
should be encouraged to read from a wide range of sources
such as books, novels, magazines and within reason, even

newspapers. In particular, efforts could be made to introduce our boys to information sources that contain examples of positive role models in society. Also, information sources that highlight the uniqueness and greatness of Africa and African culture, history, geography and society in general could be shared. Opportunities to celebrate and go deeper into topics like ancient African and contemporary black history should be taken and not allowed to be dominated by limitations of society such as that which says only one month is suitable for Black History month.

Finally, parents should start this process at a young age. As much as possible, parents should spend time with their children when they are watching television, using electronic devices such as tablets and video games and listening to music. As children get older, they will value their privacy more, but parents should still take an active interest in what their boys are listening to and watching and if necessary, act authoritatively to remove or alter the source if inappropriate. In these instances, conversations should be held as to why the parent took these measures and how the child feels about this decision.

Principle 7

Relationships - Teach them to choose wisely who they allow to board their ship for life's journey!

IMAGINE YOU ARE on a ship. You have a destination in mind that you want to reach. You set sail on the ocean after careful planning, making sure to carry the resources you need to sustain yourself in all ways for the journey. You know there will be things along the way that might affect your journey. You may encounter storms or heavy winds. Your ship may encounter structural problems. Your health might even experience ups and downs. This is what our lives and, of course, the lives of our children are like. In the beginning of our children's lives, they live on our ship. Our journey is their journey and vice versa. As they get older, their destinations may differ from yours and they hopefully set out on their own ship, with the hope that they are successful and your paths cross as often as possible while still maintaining independence. As a parent, you do the best you can to ensure that when the time inevitably comes, your children are as prepared as possible to have a healthy and productive journey of their own.

Now imagine, while on your ship - your vessel for your journey through life - you come across another sailor who is also sailing. For whatever reasons, you decide to spend time together sailing life's journey. There are several options at this point. You can both sail the same path but with your ships unattached. From time to time, you either board their ship or they board yours but you both maintain your own ships which journey separately. Or you can have your ships linked together to effectively become one ship. You both are now travelling on the different ships which are linked together closely but at any point in time you can decouple the two vessels and sail your separate ways. Finally, in the ultimate act of trust and commitment, you can seek to let one ship go and you both sail on the same one ship. Now you are dependent on each other.

The anecdotal story just described above of course was used to paint a symbolic picture of the various forms relationships can take between two people. It is this time when the decision to partner with others, whether platonic or romantic, that our children need to be best educated and prepared for. In order to establish a base for what our sons should be looking for in a partner, it is useful to look at relationships that have been solid to stand the strongest challenges for some iconic great men of African-descent in our recent past. Three good examples of this that I will be using as case studies are Betty Shabazz - wife of Malcolm X, Amy Jacques Garvey - wife of Marcus Garvey and Coretta Scott King - wife of Reverend Dr Martin Luther King. These three women went through some of the most challenging experiences not just as individuals but also as wives and, of course, experiences that were inclusive of their respective families including their children. (Betty Shabazz had six children (daughters), Amy Jacques Garvey had two sons, Coretta Scott King had four children.)

Betty Shabazz and Malcolm X[22]

One of Betty Shabazz's most powerful qualities was her devotion to filling her role as wife and partner despite the rollercoaster that life would have been like with her well-known and loved but often outspoken and controversial husband Malcolm X, later known as El Hajj Malik Shabazz. Books written about her life suggest her commitment and patience must have been tried severely and on many occasions over the course of her marriage to Malcolm, from which she bore six children. Life as wife to Malcolm X, the personality and not necessarily the man himself, would have been particularly difficult during those times her family would have been placed in direct danger due to the public nature of her husband as a political and religious personality, whose opinions often conflicted with those of other very powerful people and organizations. Despite having to deal with things such as these threats against his life, the resultant potential danger for herself and her children and the frequent absence of her husband on long trips, Betty Shabazz would remain devoted to him to the very end. Tragically, Betty Shabazz and her and Malcolm's children were present there on that fateful day when his life would be taken by the bullets of assassins, a saddening but strong testament to the devotion that she embodied as a wife.

Amy Jacques Garvey[23]

Amy Jacques Garvey is remembered for her tireless work as not only a supporter of Marcus Garvey's UNIA movement but

---

[22] *For more information on Betty Shabazz, see Rickford, Russell John. Betty Shabazz: A Remarkable Story of Survival and Faith before and after Malcolm X. Naperville, Ill.: Sourcebooks, 2003.*

[23] *For more information on Amy Jacques Garvey see Taylor, Ula Yvette. The Veiled Garvey: The Life and Times of Amy Jacques Garvey. The University of California, Santa Barbara 1992.*

also as an ardent participant. She was known for being a fiery speaker in her own right so much so that some say at times she was potentially seen as a threat to Marcus Garvey's leadership of the organization. It is this quality of having shared her husband's passion and zeal for a larger purpose that is extremely admirable and valuable in regards to the example that can be learned by our boys of African-descent for their relationships to come. It is largely through Amy Garvey's meticulous record keeping of the work and words of her husband that our current generation can know what a momentous orator he was and what a powerful message towards self-determination that he preached especially when the goings on of that particular time period are considered. An avid writer herself, Amy Garvey was a contributor to the official newspaper of the UNIA, *Negro World*, and through this medium she would clearly outline her vision of women as both reliable and passionate supporters of their husbands but also as capable leaders and visionaries themselves. In the latter stages of their marriage, Amy Garvey would show both her devotion by traveling with Marcus Garvey to his place of birth, Jamaica, after he was deported there from the United States as well as demonstrate her personal intellect and leadership through the continuing on the work of pan-Africanism in her own stead despite an eventual move abroad to England by Marcus Garvey. This would include the publication of several works, including books of her own pen as well as a 3rd volume of the classic, coveted and well-known book series *Philosophy and Opinions of Marcus Garvey*.

Coretta Scott King and Martin Luther King Jr

Many words could be used to characterize Coretta Scott King but the two words I will use are grace and poise! History records that Coretta Scott King was a talented musician and had strong academic prowess that would lead her to be a pioneer in the teaching field that at that time was very difficult for non-whites to enter due to the strong racial segregationist's' policies of the day. It is also said that Martin Luther King Jr, son of a very well established and popular minister and an obvious prospective husband for many a woman in his generation, knew within a short time of meeting Coretta Scott that she would be his future wife! From the moment they were married, the King Jr family would become embroiled in the Civil Rights struggle. With the grace and poise that she possessed in bundles naturally, Coretta Scott King would take on the role of wife and mother to the highly influential and public figure that her husband would become from those very earliest of days of her marriage. Over the course of their marriage, her husband would spend many a night not just away from the family but also jailed for his non-violent actions meant to prick America's conscious in regard to the blatant systems of segregation and inequality that characterized the South in particular at that time. What is particularly striking about the relationship between Coretta Scott King and Martin Luther King Jr is how spirited she was in ensuring that her husband never forgot his family despite his huge task of leading the civil rights movement.

• • •

Using these examples of some of our notable great black men of history and their wives, what core characteristics can be drawn out in terms of relationships that can serve to provide guidance to our boys of African-descent at that critical stage of life when they will choose a companion? From the examples of the lives of the incredible women cited above, for me, several core principles stand out that seemed central to not only ensuring the marriages of the women were successes but also that the great works of their husband were able to be sustained so that their memories and legacies live on even to this day. These principles are:

- devotion, loyalty and resilience (Betty Shabazz)
- Intellect, strong-willed independence and leadership (Amy Jacques Garvey)
- beauty, grace and poise (Coretta Scott King)

Boys of African-descent should be aware that only partners who can devote themselves and their energy, be loyal and have the resilience to build, maintain and grow the types of relationships necessary to establish strong and healthy families are worth investing their time in. It is only with strong and healthy families that the African community can flourish and thrive and eventually in time work towards a greatness reflective of their past. Our boys also need to know that strength and independence in a woman is not a negative trait but rather a sign of a true leader and of a person that has the potential to build great things given the time, right resources and plenty of positive and uplifting encouragement towards her individual goals and that of a family collective. Finally, our boys need to understand that a woman's beauty, grace and poise need not be sacrificed or substituted for her innate strength and independence. African women, with all their strength and power, have also always been icons of beauty from time immemorial and even to this day, the world of fashion and cosmetics continually culturally appropriate their style.

The reality is that our boys will not instinctively know what qualities they need to look for in a potential partner that may work towards best ensuring a healthy, happy and productive relationship. This becomes obvious when statistics that can reveal the health of black relationships are considered. For example, when the divorce rates in the USA are looked at by ethnicity, it is sobering to know that it is the families of African-descent that suffer from the highest divorce rates.[24] Strong nations depend on strong communities and strong communities depend on strong families so it is no wonder that the nation of African people particularly in the West is suffering in so many ways including in the areas of health, education and economics/finances. With all this in mind, it is of the utmost importance that parents, the extended family members and even in many regards, the collective community, become involved in the education of our boys of African-descent regarding relationships and the selection of partners towards their personal and community success over the long term. This was clearly demonstrated in the relationship of Martin Luther King Jr and Coretta Scott, as it is recorded that Martin's family vigorously vetted his future partner as well Martin himself ensured that his future wife meet and spent time with his parents before they were married.

Encourage our boys of African-descent to be wise, meticulous and proscriptive in the process of forming relationships that have to the potential to be long-lasting in their lives. Ensure that they look at the positive and solid examples around them of relationships that have worked and use them as models for that which will also be fruitful for the own

---

[24] www.washingtonpost.com/news/wonk/wp/2016/04/06/who-gets-divorced-in-america-in-7-charts/?noredirect=on

success. In particular, let them know that 'prevention is better than the cure' and it pays to put in place planning and have a high-quality standard for one of the most important factors many of us will ever have in our lives, that of, our life partner. This is particularly important when it comes to the values that the individual holds about family, gender roles, spirituality, diet and lifestyle and critically – economics and finances.

Principle 8

Goal Planning - Even the best archer cannot hit a target he has not seen.

THIS PRINCIPLE ALLUDES to a metaphor of our boys of African-descent ultimately being akin to marksmen who are in pursuit of many targets in life, specifically those targets that they will eventually identify as life goals. The act of marksmanship is very different depending on what you are trying to hit, what you want to hit the target with and the environmental conditions that you and the target are in. However, despite these differences the rules of effective marksmanship are the same for many marksmen, regardless of the sport or activity, and similarly, employing these rules in the process of our boys seeking to achieve their targets and goals in life can aid them in assuring this is accomplished efficiently and effectively.

The rules of effective marksmanship can be summarized as:

1: Sighting and alignment must be correct, inclusive of environmental considerations.
2: The marksman must point naturally at the target without any undue physical effort.

3: Position and hold must be firm enough to support dis-
    charge aimed at target.

4: Discharge must be released and followed through
    without disturbing the position.

Let's look more closely at these rules of marksmanship and how they can be applied by our boys of African-descent to achieve success in their lives and reach their individual goals.

Rule #1 -: *Sighting and Alignment.*

Notice the number one rule, *'sighting and alignment* must be correct'. This relates to the critical act of goal planning for our young sons of African-descent so that they can success-fully hit the targets they set for themselves towards their success, the collective success of their family and ultimately, the African nation. For you to successfully hit your target, you must have sight of where it is. This is the fundamental and first rule in marksmanship and likewise, this must be the fun-damental principle that we teach our sons to hold to in their pursuit of success in life. To have sight of your target (aka your goals), you must first know what your target/goals are. Goal planning through interrogating one's skills, purpose and pas-sions is a very powerful step in the visualization and actual-ization process that will allow our boys of African-descent to change their realities through self-determination.

Visualization is the act of going within one's mind and using not the physical eye of the body, but the inner eye of the mind, to see what goals a person may want or need to achieve in life. It is a common saying that 'the mind is like a sponge' and so what the mind of our boys of African-descent are exposed to will determine to a large extent what imagery and prospective goals that they might visualize and then look to obtain. Therefore it is important, if not critical, that the minds of our children be focused and centered on those things that will ultimately empower and uplift them, their family and their communities. Collectively, this process of knowing what will empower and uplift oneself is colloquially called 'gaining knowledge of Self' and is a process that can be facilitated by encouraging our boys to learn their history and culture through self-education and spending time with Elders as well as to spend personal time reflecting on who they are in relation to the past, present and the future.

As a next step towards successful goal planning, once our boys are pursuing 'knowledge of Self' and are actively visualizing what steps they may need to take to actualize their goals, the act of writing down these goals becomes important. I personally advocate the <u>act of keeping and writing in a journal (colloquially called 'journaling')</u> by young people, starting from around the teenage years. Having a personal journal is a powerful tool that can aid in the process of exploring and gaining 'knowledge of Self', the visualization of potential goals through brainstorming and recording thoughts and ideas as well as officially recording targets and goals that a boy may set for himself in line with his developing life plan. When keeping a journal, every time an entry is made, it should be dated, as this allows the journal keeper to look back in reflection on what their previous mindset, goals or events in their life would have been like. A journal and all that goes into it is private and confidential and young people need to know that inside the confines of their personal journal pages are a safe space where they can freely and independently express whatever thoughts, ideas and feelings come to mind. This ensures that their visualization and reflective process is not limited or restricted in any way, which will allow them to unlock, reach into and then access their individuality and uniqueness.

Rule #2 - Point naturally at your target.

Life goals should not be plucked randomly from the air nor should they be dictated to our boys of African-descent based on the desire of others' expectations, wants, needs or desires. Rather, their goals should be those that arise as a result of the coming together of their passions, purpose and interest as well as seasoned by their personal life experiences. This reality relates directly to the second rule of effective marksmanship which is the marksman, once the target is identified, needs to point naturally at his target. The goals that our boys set are for them, not for us. Experienced parents know that any young person forced to pursue a dream or goal that is not truly theirs and that they do not believe in is bound to not commit fully to that pursuit and as a result not reach their full potential.

The act of writing down goals has a profound effect on making a goal a reality. It allows you to orientate yourself towards the target so you can start to move towards it. If you cannot see it, you cannot believe it will happen and the act of writing down a goal allows a person to not only have to visualize it mentally but also is the first step towards physically manifesting that goal, albeit on a piece of paper. As a man thinketh, so shall it be! What type of goals should our boys of African-descent be planning? One very effective strategy is to ask our young people to set out a 1-year, 3-year, 5-year and 10-year plan. This allows them to consider not just the immediate future but also the long term one and what steps need to be in place to make their long-term plan happen. These time-sensitive plans should be discussed at length with the young person and advice and guidance delivered as appropriate. This advice and guidance should not attempt to stifle the creativity, independence and uniqueness shown by our young boys if the steps they take may not match with what we personally feel they should be looking at. Rather, young people should be encouraged to reactively monitor and review their goals on a regular basis (yearly) and make changes accordingly as life inevitably teaches them lessons along the way. Their birthdays or the start of a new year are excellent times to have such regular review cycles.

Rule #3 - Hold must be firm enough to support.
This rule can be likened to the necessary resilience that our boys of African-descent will inevitably need to have in the long-term process of achieving their goals. The best things in life are often those that take hard work and sacrifice to obtain; this means the process to obtaining success can be difficult. However, the reward upon holding firm until that goal is achieved is always sweet and worth it in the long run. The higher our boys set their targets and goals, the more resilience and staying power they will need in order to accomplish them. Of course, at times, they will also need the support of their parents, extended family as well as the support of the greater village. This support is especially true for goals that go beyond the value of rewarding the individual such as those that take into account collective family or community progress. Along with individualistic goals that seek to satisfy the inner purpose and passion of our boys of African-descent, as they mature and become secure in who they are, they

hopefully will be encouraged to also put into motion target setting that includes these larger minded goals. Importantly, our boys should be strongly encouraged to seek out advice from those who have experience in the various fields of endeavors they may be pursuing and, in the process, build up strong networks of contacts and links that can help to further facilitate their long-term success.

Rule #4 - Discharge must be released and followed through. At some point, goals and targets either get achieved or realizations may come whereby it is clearly seen that a target or goal may not be able to be accomplished. The inevitable release of these unattainable goals must take place so that room for redeveloped goals and renewed purpose can start. Even for those goals accomplished, our boys of African-descent should always be encouraged to aim higher and broader as one success is encountered. Once one target is acquired or a goal obtained, that is a clear signal that another should be identified in respect of their life's passion and purpose and sought out for.

Follow through is a critical skill that our boys must develop and be nurtured in and along with its cousin – self-discipline – it is unfortunately one quality that is severely lacking in many of today's younger generations and the cause of much of the lack of progress of boys of African-descent as individuals and as a collective group. Follow through is equivalent to the values of perseverance, diligence and steadfastness. There is a saying that goes *"Hard work beats talent when talent fails to work hard"*. This saying and the learning point within it is memorialized in the story of the tortoise and hare. Of course, the hare was more naturally talented with the physical attributes needed to win the race, but the tortoise possessed the mental fortitude and the qualities spoken about above - perseverance, diligence and steadfastness – that eventually would prove to be the deciding factor in him winning the race.

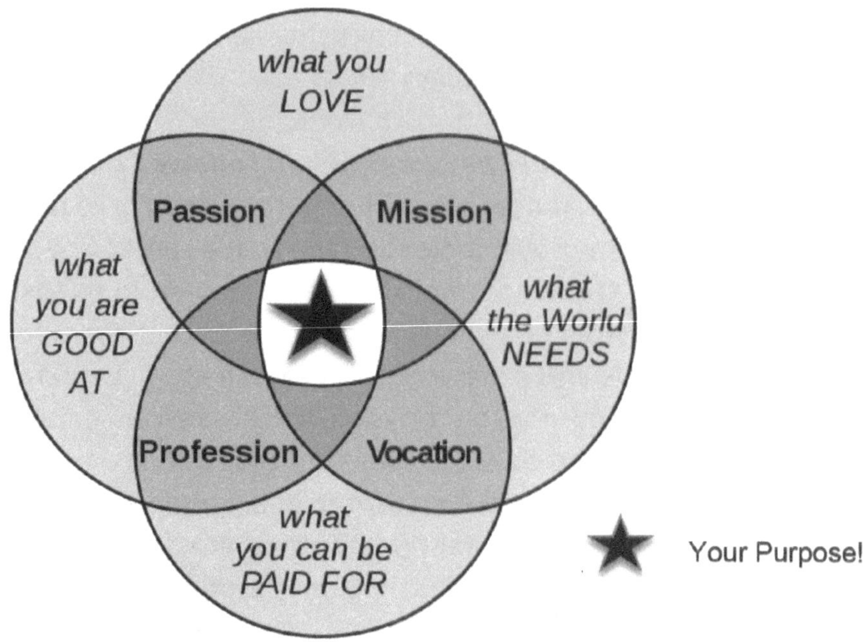

Venn diagram on how to find one's true purpose[25]

In closing this chapter on the importance of determining one's key goals in life and how to most effectively ensure these goals are achieved, it is helpful to reflect on the following quote: "a rudderless ship can only head where the winds may take it." In simple terms, having goals allows our young boys of African-descent to be masters of their own destiny

25 Wikimedia Commons, https://commons.wikimedia.org/wiki/File:Ikigai-EN.svg [Accessed 17/06/2019]

and to set the course for their life that will most benefit them. As the Venn diagram above shows, in order to find one's purpose, there are four core questions that one can potentially consider. Wrongly identifying the answer to any one of these questions can be disastrous as it would mean the inability to hit that center 'sweet spot' where all four factors line up in symmetry and synergy. Using a mindful approach to setting goals in life, considering one's profession, vocation, passion and mission can help our boys to move closer to their true purpose and, in the long run, led a truly fulfilling life that leaves no regret at its final call.

Principle 9

Love is spelled T.I.M.E. - Love is shown with presence, not money.

AS A DAD of six children, but with two who do not live with me, I intimately know that the most important gift you can give a child is <u>not material things or physical possessions</u>. The most important and valuable gift is that of your **time**. Love is shown most deeply not by the act of purchasing and providing material things but by sacrificing your most precious resource given to us all, which is our time.

Now, make no mistake - provision of finances and/or other material resources for our children is critical. No woman should be left willingly to raise a child on her own financially when it took a man AND woman to create that life. Too often in our community, we hear about the ideas of 'deadbeat dads' - a term used to refer to men who have become fathers but usually provide no support financially, materially or physically by presence towards the upbringing of their children. Where these types of fathers exist, they should be educated so as to help develop more responsible behaviors or if this not possible, removed from the child's life until they are able to contribute as a father to the raising of their children in a productive manner in some form or fashion.

Again, making a substantive contribution to a child's life does not have to be in the form of money or materials if this is not possible, but can and should be first in the form of a father's presence. The physical act of being there for a child for their inevitable ups and downs, being able to place an arm around that child to say you love them and even when direct physical presence is not possible, that child being able to contact the father via phone or letter and vice versa goes a long way to letting that child know you as a father love and care for them. It is only through having a foundation of positive interaction with children in their early years through father and son that the child can then go on to ensure that they foster and develop a positive relationship with their sons in the future. This chain of positive fatherhood within a lineage is critical if our African nation is to thrive over time and for the dysfunction within the African family unit, particularly in the African diaspora, is to begin to dissipate.

These assertions are not just conjecture. There is much research to back these claims up. One such conglomeration of research was published by the University of Guelph in 2007.[26] The study shows countless areas where having fatherly involvement in a child's life has positive impacts from the very early stages of a child's life including on the cognitive development of infants. The impact of a father's presence carries on into the emotional development and wellbeing of a child in

---

[26] http://www.fira.ca/cms/documents/29/Effects_of_Father_Involvement.pdf

their later years as well as towards their social development and physical health.

However, it is not just research studies that I have to convince me of the importance of being a present and involved father. It's also my own experiences. I grew up in a single parent household, being raised by my mother after my mother and dad divorced when I was a young age. To this day, I do not know much about why they chose to separate and then divorce but I do know it has an impact on me even now. Remembering how much I wanted my father to be a part of my life definitely inspired me to attempt to ensure that any children I have would not have to have the same wants and desires I did. I would be there for them! I also remember the disappointment when those inevitable moments come when your father does not turn up to be there for whatever reasons there may be. No matter the reason, as a child, this absence leads to disappointment and disappointment can lead to resentment. Resentment in turn, if left unexplored and unresolved, can then lead to further dysfunction in one's own relationships with both partners and children thus creating a cycle of dysfunction.

I am thankful that the impact of not having my father directly in my presence in the home as I grew up did not destroy the potential for having a positive relationship with my father eventually. As I became older and more independent, I sought out his advice and company when I could, and he reciprocated these actions. This mean that we now have a positive and healthy relationship where we can show affection to each other, discuss the things that we both find interesting and also my own children can enjoy having a grandfather that they can spend time with when possible. However, despite my best efforts, the cycle of having a fatherless home that I experienced has also now affected some of my own children, as they have had to live with my own personal experience of being separated from their mother. How much of the separation that I experienced in my personal adult life from my partners may have been avoided if I was raised in a happy, healthy and loving home with both my mother AND father will never be known. However, there is a large body of research that shows negative impacts are more likely to occur as a result of being a child who has experienced divorce, separation of their parents and/or living in a single parent home.[27]

So, if children measure love through time spent, how and what should parents do in order to maximize the value gained through this time spent together? There are five key principles that can be used to bring the best out of boys of African-descent through time spent together: *affection, listening, interaction, structure and fun.* Let's start with affection, as this should form the basis of the relationship between parent and child. Let's start with affection. **Affection** means the explicit showing of love to the child, no matter the age. Touching in the form of hugs, high fives, handshakes, wrestling or whatever is appropriate and normal to you and your child is extremely important as it solidifies the bond between the parent and child as well as allows spiritual (inner) energy to flow between them. This exchange of energy helps to transfer emotions of positivity, trust and happiness between child and parent which acts like a food to nourish the soul of the child and nurture his wellbeing.

---

[27]   *The impact of family structure on the health of children: Effects of divorce https://www.ncbi.nlm.nih.gov/pmc/articles/PMC4240051/*

Listening is also key. Any child not listened to will become frustrated and eventually may even seek other sources that they feel will listen to them and as we all know, many of these alternative ears may not have the child's best interest at heart. When listening, attention should be paid on being an active listener. That is a listener who is actively interested in what the boy has to say, why they are seeing it and what they are saying means. Being a good listener to our young boys of African-descent means that they feel comfortable sharing with us those things that they feel are valuable to them and this then give us the opportunity to either reinforce those things or constructively provide feedback on how or what might need to change in the scenarios they present to us.

Interaction refers to the act of being involved with our boys, again at any age. In this age of smart phones and ubiquitous technological saturation, it is all too easy for everyone to shrink into their own personal bubble with very little interaction between them. This of course then creates a vacuum in which the beneficial values that should be shared between parents and child are not transmitted and instead these values and information are gained from the digital sources that our young people are invariably locked into in modern times. For our boys of African-descent, spending time with male role models of integrity and value cannot be overstated. Of course, a boys' father should be the prime example in this regard but if a biological father figure is not present, then efforts should be made to ensure that a surrogate male is able and willing. This is even more important in the development of our young boys who gain value from seeing and interacting with strong, positive male role models who they then in turn can seek to model their own lives around.

Structure refers to ensuring that our young boys are using their time wisely and in a balanced way that promotes their development mentally, educationally, physically and spiritually. Having structure in a boy's life provides a backbone on which development can take place and actually creates more usable space and time for free activities in an effective and balanced manner than an unstructured lifestyle. Efforts should be made by the parents of our young boys of African-descent to ensure they have and are informed on a set structure for their week, one that includes time being spent together. Aspects such as family time, chores, academics (revision and homework), physical activities such as sports and leisure and recreation activities should all be built in to this structure and the schedule shared and displayed in the boy's personal space. Older boys should be encouraged to create and develop as well as self-regulate their own activity schedule throughout the week.

The last but probably most important aspect of spending time with our boys of African-descent is to make sure there is time for **fun**. Of course, there needs to be structured time when we are assisting them to work towards some specific goal in a very focused manner but there also needs to be balance between the time we interact with them in a fun way so that they actually enjoy their parent's company. All of us know that we gravitate towards those things that make us feel good. This has a biological reason as the brain releases a hormone called dopamine that creates a feel-good factor in our body when we are doing something we enjoy. We like the way dopamine make us feel so we keep going back for more! So if we recognize that we have some very important life lessons to teach our children, in particular our young boys of African-descent, we need to ensure that their experiences with us are fun so that they return regularly to receive the wisdom that we so desperately need to impart.

Principle 10

His God Within - "and darkness was upon the face of the deep. And the Spirit of God moved upon the face of the waters."
Genesis 1:2

THIS PASSAGE IS one of the most powerful but not easily understood allegories within the collection of stories, traditions and lessons we call the Bible. If thought about deeply, the passage is relating how a deep and dark water provided a medium for the very spirit of the Creator to travel upon and to begin the creative process. Contradictorily, having dark skin, and to be considered "black", has often been used as a way to degrade, discriminate or oppress those people that are of African-descent. For people of African-descent, and for our boys in particular, this passage can be a source of inspiration towards unlocking an appreciation for the power of the Divine, i.e. creation, that lies within us all. When the source of "our blackness" is fully understood, we can then begin to make connections between both the phenotype of dark skin and the genetic source code that facilitates not only the exterior expression of this creative power but also the ability to uniquely connect with our Universe.

The biological molecule that provides the physiological basis for dark skin is called melanin and is actually a source of power that our boys should see as a gift and definitely not as a curse. Melanin is a biochemical produced by special cells in our body called melanocytes. Melanin is produced by melanocytes both due to normal hormonal biosynthesis in our bodies on an on-going basis as well as can be produced upon stimulation by UV light such as that which radiates from the Sun. In the skin, melanin acts as a pigment and is black in appearance. This black appearance is caused by melanin's ability to absorb the visible wavelengths of the electromagnetic spectrum that emanates from light energy sources like the sun. Melanin also absorbs parts of the electromagnetic spectrum that we cannot see with our naked eye, in particular that of UV-B[28] light rays. This absorption of UV-B light has a protective role for our body. UV light can damage the DNA of cells, damage which can lead to cancer, and the melanin molecules of our skin act as an absorbent shield against these harmful rays.

Melanin is not just present in our skin but is present in varying amounts around many areas of our body and plays a critical role in not only keeping us healthy but also allowing our bodies to sense and interact with the world around us. One powerful instance of this is the role that melanin plays in the brain. In the parts of the brain that scientists have found to be responsible for many physiological functions including

---

[28] UV stands for ultra-violet light which is light radiating at a particular wavelength (10 nanometers to 400 nanometers) on the electromagnetic spectrum.

movement and coordination, melanin is seen to play a key role. In fact, the name of this part of the brain is the 'substantia nigra' which literally translates from Latin as the "black substance" and this black color in this area results from the presence of a form of melanin. Melanin also plays a key role in both the function of the eye and the ear. In the eye, melanin is thought to not only play a protective role against disease similar to that which it plays in the skin but also an important part of the ability of the retina of the eye to function effectively.[29] In the ear, melanocytes and the production of melanin has been found to influence the ear's communication to the brain in regards to balance.[30] Melanin is also seen to play a very important protective role from a physiological standpoint. Individuals with more melanin present in the inner ear were shown to have less susceptibility to hearing loss as well as a greater sensitivity to sound.[31]

Besides the role melanin plays in the skin, the brain, the eyes and the ears, there are many, many more vital functions that this amazing molecule plays in the body. Our boys of African-descent should be taught about why their skin complexion is different and learn to value the life-enhancing

---

[29] *Ophthalmologe. 2001 Dec; 98(12):1181-5. Characteristics and functions of melanin in retinal pigment epithelium. [Article in German] Peters S¹, Schraermeyer U.*

[30] *Hu, D., Simon, J. D. and Sarna, T. (2008), Role of Ocular Melanin in Ophthalmic Physiology and Pathology†. Photochemistry and Photobiology, 84: 639-644. doi:10.1111/j.1751-1097.2008.00316.x*

[31] *Carlie Driscoll, Joseph Kei, Steven Arnold, Dominic Doherty, John Krajewski, Greer McDonald, Ellen McKeering, Mikaela Tyrrell & Bradley McPherson (2009) Racial Heritage/Melanin and Otoacoustic Emission Measures of Cochlear Function, Asia Pacific Journal of Speech, Language and Hearing, 12:1, 1-12, DOI: 10.1179/jslh.2009.12.1.1*

benefits that being of darker skin and possessing valuable DNA that encodes for melanin production accords them. Just as allegorically the spirit of God moved upon the face of deep and dark waters before the act of creation begin, let's establish a consciousness within our boys that teaches them to see opportunity for them to be creators in their own right on a daily basis as the life-giving energy of the Sun moves upon the darkness of their own skin.

Walter Williams, a rigorous researcher and publisher of books associated with the African-centered genre, encouraged people of African-descent to reflect on four essential questions when looking for the deeper meaning of life and our existence.[32] He called these questions the four mysteries and stated that no one can ever answer these questions with complete authority due to the inherent unobtainability of the answers being sought. These questions are: one - where did life come from, two - where does the human spirit go after death, three - how did the first human woman and man come to be, and four - where does the soul that brings personal consciousness to a human embryo come from?

For Walter Williams, it was not that asking oneself these questions is wrong. What was wrong in his eyes was both the amount of time people of African-descent would spend searching for answers to questions that where impossible to answer while at the same time the amount of blind faith and trust that people put into human individuals no different

---

[32] *Christianity and the Moors Walter Williams and Clemson Brown Christianity Then and Now, https://www.youtube.com/watch?v=VUl Amx7wq9s&list=PLRT6OfPSGhJRH0aeT1WxfRrwCHjEyPMij&index=9 &safe=active*

than them or religious systems created by man to provide an answer. Instead, he suggests, rather than looking outside of oneself for the answers surrounding the mystery of life, it is important to realize that every human being is born with their own innate spirituality and a unique and personal connection to the Divine source from which all things came. Before we are influenced by the opinions and beliefs of the societies we live in, as babies born from our mother's wombs, we carry no preconceived notions of how we can connect with and appreciate the universe we were born into. This inborn state of mind over time becomes influenced by religion and by learned behaviors and ways of thinking we learn from others.

In seeking a higher purpose and a deeper connection with the Universe and with their own innate divine spirituality, our boys of African-descent should be taught of the existence of an inborn, natural connection they have with life, the Universe and existence itself. All matter and energy had to come from somewhere and ultimately this prime source is the origin of us all, inclusive of our physical being and our immaterial consciousness. With the passage of time, all of creation has transpired in its infinite complexity to interact in ways understood and known and in manners still unknown or not understood to at some point result in the formation of our existence. As products of this divine algorithm of existence and creation, our boys should be made to appreciate that they have a personal, intimate and direct connection to the Divine source and also play an important role in the continual transmission of the divine energy and matter that makes up their being and consciousness across eternity. In seeking answers to the divine, one need only listen to the Divine within – that sacred voice that speaks to us all.

As our unique genetic code has been passed down to us through the living organisms that were our mothers, fathers and grand-ancestors, in the same way the unique genetic code of the original Creator has also been passed down through the eons of time to give rise to our existence today. Reproduction then can be seen as the penultimate achievement of any and all life forms. It ensures that the unique, priceless and sacred genetic material of an organism can be passed on to a new generation who hopefully can continue the cycle of life of our species. When our boys of African-descent understand not only the power they have by having the ability to reproduce but also the responsibility that comes with it, they can then move into a state of divine consciousness whereby they can fully understand themselves as Creators possessive of the true spirit of God allegorically spoken about in the Bible's very first verses.

Final Words

What is brilliance and why should it be unlocked in our boys of African-descent?

THE WORD 'BRILLIANCE' literally means shining and etymologically stems from the root word 'beryl', which means "precious stone". As we know precious stones are those that hold immense value not only for their beauty but for their attributes and properties which make them incredibly useful in a multitude of applications. The value of precious stones increases due to their rare nature and the fact that even when unearthed, they still must be purified and polished for them to exert their maximum potential! No word then could be more suitable to describe our boys of African-descent. A rare, highly valuable resource capable of so much but necessarily needing of purification and polishing to reach their maximum potential.

Through the eons of time that embodies the time of African peoples on this earth, a multitude of systems have existed to ensure the development of this precious resource. Ethno-cultural technologies such as the range of rites of passage practices that were upheld regularly across the diverse societies living on the African continent are one such system that our boys of African-descent in the diaspora so desperately need but are severely disconnected from. Even after the devastation visited upon the social, mental and economic existence of African peoples in the West due to the trans-Atlantic slave trade and its after effects, the resilience of our traditional African values has always meant that a modicum of the guiding light of our previous ways of rites of passage existed in our family structures. Discipline, an emphasis on hardwork, progress and mental strength have always been a hallmark of our community, even during those periods when the worst was visited upon us. But modern-day society has reaped havoc on the family structure of all socio-ethnic groups, including diasporic Africans and those at home on the continent. This has meant that the family structures and traditions that might have been there previously to act as 'rites of passage' in absentia are also being degraded and more must be done to ensure that a developmental system to unlock the brilliance of our boys of African-descent is in place.

Our world, not just our insular community as African people, needs the brilliance of our boys more than ever. In areas such as leadership, both international and on local levels, there is a clarion call to have strong figures who can tackle the critical issues of today's modern world. In the arena of technology and the economy, there is an increasing awareness of the unsustainable pyramid of wealth concentration in the hands of a very, very small elite while the masses have to survive on much less. We need the brilliant minds of our boys to unlock the spirit of entrepreneurship that has always existed inside of us as a people and to develop new pathways to wealth and financial sustainability that can help redress the wealth imbalance. Our global environment is also crying out for solutions to a range of issues threatening to make our world potentially inhabitable for future generations, or at best, a far cry from the richly, diverse world that past generations were able to enjoy. It is with their unique view points and their vast untapped potential that potential solutions to these types of crises can be proposed and the tipping point towards irreversible environmental degradation be averted.

But while these issues on the macro scale loom as crucial regarding the need to unlock the brilliance of our boys of African-descent, perhaps it is the micro-scale issues that they are needed the most on. Issues revolving around the black family and its sustainability and, even more important, whether the black man's ongoing existence will be as a significant player on the world stage or one resigned to the peanut gallery of the world's societies. One thing is for certain, while we need a new generation of Marcus Garvey's, Elijah Muhammad's, Martin Delaney's, Matthew Henson's, Benjamin Banneker's and Imhotep's for our world, both present and future, the source will rely as much on harnessing the ancient Akan principle of 'sankofa' – that is, to look backwards in order to know where you are going – in addition to teaching our boys at their very core to embody that of 'nyansapo' – the wisdom that stems from their ingenious within.